MATH SMARTS!

Pre-Algebra
and
Algebra
SMARTS!

Lucille Caron
Philip M. St. Jacques

Enslow Publishers, Inc.
40 Industrial Road
Box 398
Berkeley Heights, NJ 07922
USA

http://www.enslow.com

Original edition published as *Pre-Algebra and Algebra* in 2000.

Library of Congress Cataloging-in-Publication Data

Caron, Lucille.
  Pre-algebra and algebra smarts! / Lucille Caron and Philip M. St. Jacques.
      p. cm. — (Math smarts!)
  Summary: "Re-inforce classroom learning of important pre-algebra and
algebra skills such as positive and negative rational numbers, absolute value,
and solving equations"— Provided by publisher.
  Includes index.
  ISBN 978-0-7660-3938-4
  1. Mathematics—Juvenile literature. 2. Algebra—Juvenile literature.
  I. St. Jacques, Philip M. II. Title.
  QA107.2.C35 2012
  512.9—dc22

                                                                2011006928

Paperback ISBN 978-1-59845-319-5

Printed in China

052011 Leo Paper Group, Heshan City, Guangdong, China.

10 9 8 7 6 5 4 3 2 1

To Our Readers: We have done our best to make sure all Internet addresses
in this book were active and appropriate when we went to press. However, the
author and the publisher have no control over and assume no liability for the
material available on those Internet sites or on other Web sites they may link to.
Any comments or suggestions can be sent by e-mail to comments@enslow.com
or to the address on the back cover.

Cover Illustration: Shutterstock.com

Contents

Introduction

If you were to look up the meaning of the word *mathematics*, you would find that it is the study of numbers, quantities, and shapes, and how they are related to each other.

Mathematics is very important to all world cultures, including our world of work. The following are just some of the ways in which studying math will help you:

▶ You will know how much money you are spending at the store.

▶ You will know if the cashier has given you enough change.

▶ You will know how to use measurements to build things.

▶ Your science classes will be easier and more interesting.

▶ You will understand music on a whole new level.

▶ You will be empowered to qualify for and land a rewarding job.

Algebra is a branch of mathematics. It uses the same basic operations that you have learned: addition, subtraction, multiplication, and division. However, algebra deals with properties of numbers using symbols.

People need to know algebra to find out if they received the correct change at the store. Engineers use algebra to set the timing of different traffic lights on a street or to design the shape of a sports ball.

This book has been written so that you can learn about pre-algebra at your own speed. It will help you get prepared for your future study of algebra. You can use this book on your own, or work together with a friend, tutor, or parent.

Good luck and have fun!

Algebra helps us understand mathematics in a general way. In algebra, letters represent numbers—including whole numbers, integers, and rational numbers. Mathematical rules, though, still apply.

So that you can see why algebra works and how it applies to real life, let's review the different kinds of numbers, their operations, and the properties of their operations.

Whole Numbers and Integers

Whole numbers consist of the counting numbers and zero.

Whole Numbers: 0, 1, 2, 3, 4, 5, 6, 7, 8, 9, 10, 11, 12, . . .

We can represent whole numbers on a number line.

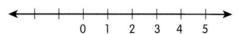

All the whole numbers, except for zero, are called positive integers. Zero is an integer, but it is neither positive nor negative. We can represent positive integers on the number line by placing a positive sign (+) before each whole number. A positive sign indicates that the number is larger than zero.

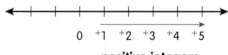

positive integers

Numbers smaller than zero are called negative integers. We can represent negative integers on the number line by placing a negative sign (−) before each number.

negative integers

Whole numbers are the counting numbers and zero: 0, 1, 2, 3, 4, 5, 6, ...
Integers are the counting numbers, the negative of these, and zero: . . .
⁻3, ⁻2, ⁻1, 0, 1, 2, 3, . . .

Reading and Writing Integers

A ⁻4 is read, "Negative four." The symbol is placed on the upper left of the numeral. The negative and positive signs are raised to distinguish them from the signs for the operation of addition (plus, +) and subtraction (minus, −).

Four units to the left of zero on a number line are shown.

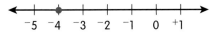

A ⁺4 is read, "Positive four." The number 4 is a whole number. We can read the number 4 as "four" or "positive four." If the positive sign (+) is not written before a number, the number is understood to be positive.

Opposites

Opposites are pairs of numbers that are the same distance away from zero, but on opposite sides. Every number has only one opposite.

Look at the number line. The opposite of ⁻2 is ⁺2.

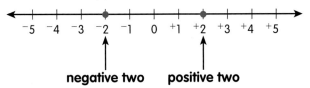

Notice that ⁻2 and ⁺2 are the same distance away from zero. The ⁻2 is two units to the left of zero while the ⁺2 is two units to the right of zero. These pairs of numbers are opposites.

Numbers greater than zero are **positive** and are to the right of zero on a number line. Numbers less than zero are **negative** and are to the left of zero on a number line.

A rational number is a number that can be written as a fraction. They include positive and negative whole numbers, mixed numerals, repeating decimals, and terminating decimals. Zero is also a rational number. Some examples of rational numbers are:

$$\frac{4}{1} \qquad \frac{125}{100} \qquad 0.\overline{6} \qquad 0.75$$

Number Line

Positive rational numbers are represented by a positive sign (+). A positive sign indicates that the number is greater than zero.

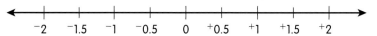

Negative rational numbers are represented by a negative sign (−). A negative sign indicates that the number is smaller than zero. The points labeled $^+0.5$ and $^-0.5$ are opposites.

$^+0.5$ is 0.5 units to the right of zero.
$^-0.5$ is 0.5 units to the left of zero.

These two points are opposites because they are the same distance from zero but on opposite sides of zero.

rational number—A number that can be written as a fraction.
Rational numbers have opposites just like integers do.

Writing a Whole Number as a Rational Number

To write a whole number as a rational number, place the whole number over one. For example, to write 6 as a rational number, place the whole number over one. $\frac{6}{1}$

Writing a Mixed Numeral as a Rational Number

Write 1.25 as a rational number.

Step 1: Read the number. "One and twenty-five hundredths"

Step 2: Write the number as a whole number and a fraction. $1\frac{25}{100}$

Step 3: Change the mixed number to an improper fraction.

$$1\frac{25}{100} = \frac{1(100) + 25}{100}$$

$$= \frac{125}{100}$$

+Rational Concentration−

Play rational concentration with a family member. Make twenty cards with examples of positive and negative rational numbers. Use some of the examples below:

⁻0.9	0.9 units to the left of zero	⁻0.8	the opposite of ⁺0.8

Mix up the cards and place them facedown. Each player selects two cards. If the player has a matching pair, he or she takes another turn. If the player does not have a matching pair, he or she returns the cards in the same place facedown again. After all the cards have been taken, the player who has the most pairs wins!

Every rational number on the number line has an **opposite** except for zero.

Ordering and comparing integers is a frequently used skill. For example, engineers compare different elevations when surveying property for a new building and meteorologists use integers when reporting temperature.

The equal sign (=) and inequality symbols are used to compare numbers. The inequality symbol < means "is less than" and the symbol > means "is greater than."

Ordering Integers

We order integers from least to greatest or smallest to largest. Any number on the number line is greater than any number to its left. Let's order the following integers using a number line.

Order ⁻3, ⁺5, ⁻4, ⁺2, ⁻1, ⁺4 from least to greatest.

Step 1: Place the integers on a number line.

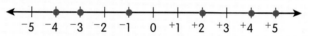

Step 2: Order the integers from least to greatest, starting with the integer on the far left on the number line.

⁻4, ⁻3, ⁻1, ⁺2, ⁺4, ⁺5

For a full table of equality and inequality symbols, see page 40.

Comparing Integers

If an integer is to the left of another integer on a number line, then use $<$ to compare the integers. If an integer is to the right of another integer, then use $>$ to compare the integers.

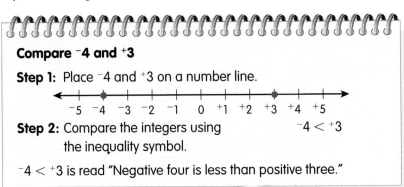

Compare $^-4$ and $^+3$

Step 1: Place $^-4$ and $^+3$ on a number line.

Step 2: Compare the integers using the inequality symbol.

$$^-4 < {}^+3$$

$^-4 < {}^+3$ is read "Negative four is less than positive three."

Look at the following examples:

Compare	In words	Inequality symbol
$^-5$ and $^-3$	$^-5$ is to the left of $^-3$	$^-5 < {}^-3$
$^+2$ and $^+1$	$^+2$ is to the right of $^+1$	$^+2 > {}^+1$
$^-4$ and $^+4$	$^-4$ is to the left of $^+4$	$^-4 < {}^+4$

Integer War

Make up at least 40 cards, each with a positive or negative integer on it. Make some cards with the same integers. Each player is given the same number of cards. All players lay down a card and compare the integers. The player who laid down the card with the greatest integer takes all the cards and places them at the bottom of his pile. If two cards are equal, war is declared. Each player in the war then places three cards facedown and a fourth card faceup. The player whose fourth card is greater wins all the cards. The player who ends up with all 40 cards wins the game.

Any integer on the number line is greater than any integer to its left.

The absolute value of an integer is the distance the integer is from zero on the number line. The absolute value symbol is written as a pair of vertical bars (| |).

Absolute Value of a Negative Integer

Find the absolute value of ⁻3 $|\text{-}3| = ?$

Step 1: Represent ⁻3 on a number line.

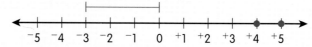

$$-5 \quad -4 \quad -3 \quad -2 \quad -1 \quad 0 \quad +1 \quad +2 \quad +3 \quad +4 \quad +5$$

Step 2: Count the number of units from 0 to ⁻3.   distance = 3 units

Step 3: Write the absolute value of negative three. $|\text{-}3| = 3$

The absolute value of any negative integer is always equal to the numerical value of the number without the sign.

Find the sum of $|-2| + |-5|$

Step 1: Find the absolute value of each addend. $|\text{-}2| = 2$
$|\text{-}5| = 5$

Step 2: Find the sum. $2 + 5 = 7$

So, $|\text{-}2| + |\text{-}5| = 7$

Absolute value is always a positive number. It is the distance the number is from zero on the number line.
For any value a: $(|a|) = a$ $(|\text{-}a|) = a$

Absolute Value of a Positive Integer

Find the absolute value of ⁺3 $|+3| = ?$

Step 1: Represent ⁺3 on a number line.

Step 2: Count the number of units from 0 to ⁺3.   distance = 3 units

Step 3: Write the absolute value of positive three. $|+3| = 3$

The absolute value of positive three represents 3 units above zero. The absolute value of any positive integer is always equal to the numerical value of the number without the sign.

Find the sum of $|+2| + |+5|$

Step 1: Find the absolute value of each addend. The addends are the numbers being added. $|-2| + |+5|$

Step 2: Find the sum. $2 + 5 = 7$

The absolute value of any positive or negative integer is the number written without the positive or negative sign.

Integers describe certain everyday situations. For example, temperatures can be above or below zero.

5 Adding Integers with Like Signs

Like integers are integers with the same sign. You can use circles to add integers with like signs. A white circle will represent a negative integer and a shaded circle will stand for a positive integer.

Adding Positive Integers

All the whole numbers except for zero are called positive integers.

Add $^+2 + {}^+3$

Step 1: Draw 2 shaded circles. ◯ ◯

Step 2: Draw 3 shaded circles. ◯ ◯ ◯

Step 3: Add all the circles. ◯ ◯ ◯ ◯ ◯

$$^+2 + {}^+3 = {}^+5$$

Adding Three or More Positive Integers

Add $^+4 + {}^+1 + {}^+6 + {}^+2$

addend addend sum

Step 1: Find the sum of the first two integers. $^+4 + {}^+1 = {}^+5$

Step 2: Add the sum to the third addend. $^+5 + {}^+6 = {}^+11$

Step 3: Add the sum in Step 2 to the fourth addend. $^+11 + {}^+2 = {}^+13$

$$^+4 + {}^+1 + {}^+6 + {}^+2 = {}^+13$$

The sum of two or more positive integers will always be positive because all the integers are positive.

Adding Negative Integers

Numbers to the left of zero on the number line are called negative integers.

Add $^-4 + {}^-1$

Step 1: Draw 4 circles. ○ ○ ○ ○

Step 2: Draw 1 circle. ○

Step 3: Add all the circles. ○ ○ ○ ○ ○

$$^-4 + {}^-1 = {}^-5$$

Adding Three or More Negative Integers

Add $^-2 + {}^-4 + {}^-3 + {}^-5$

Step 1: Find the sum of the first two integers. $^-2 + {}^-4 = {}^-6$

Step 2: Add the sum to the third addend. $^-6 + {}^-3 = {}^-9$

Step 3: Add the sum in Step 2 to the fourth addend. $^-9 + {}^-5 = {}^-14$

$$^-2 + {}^-4 + {}^-3 + {}^-5 = {}^-14$$

Three out of Five

Make up 20 cards with like signs. Place the cards facedown. Each player takes a turn and selects 5 cards and tries to make an addition equation using three out of the five cards. For example, if the five cards are $^-6$, $^-4$, $^-1$, $^-5$, and $^-10$, then he or she can make an addition equation using $^-4 + {}^-1 = {}^-5$ and keep the cards. If the player is unable to make an addition sentence, he or she shuffles the cards and places them facedown. The player with the most cards wins!

The sum of two or more negative integers is always negative.

Unlike integers are integers with different signs. Bankers and store owners add unlike integers every day when they total their accounts.

Adding Unlike Integers Using a Number Line

Add ⁺3 + ⁻5

Step 1: Starting at ⁺3, move five places to the left.

Step 2: The stopping point is ⁻2.

⁺3 + ⁻5 = ⁻2

Here is another way to add integers with unlike signs:

Step 1: Subtract the two integers.   5 − 3 = 2

Step 2: Write the answer using the sign of the integer with the greatest absolute value.

|−5| = 5 and |+3| = 3

5 > 3, so the answer will be negative: ⁻2

Sometimes there is more than one way to solve a problem. Pick the way you like best.

Review how to find **absolute value** on page 12.

Adding Unlike Integers Using Figures

You can use figures to add integers with unlike signs. A white circle will represent a negative integer and a shaded circle will stand for a positive integer.

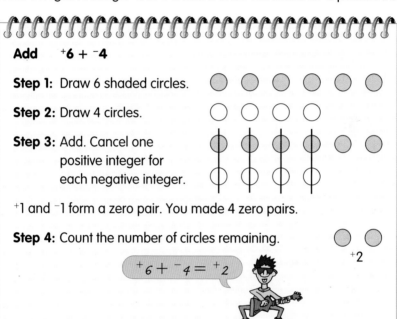

Add   +6 + ⁻4

Step 1: Draw 6 shaded circles.

Step 2: Draw 4 circles.

Step 3: Add. Cancel one positive integer for each negative integer.

⁺1 and ⁻1 form a zero pair. You made 4 zero pairs.

Step 4: Count the number of circles remaining.

+2

⁺6 + ⁻4 = ⁺2

Negative or Positive?

Play "Negative or Positive?" with a family member. You need 63 cards. Use the integers from ⁻30 to ⁺30, including zero, on the cards. Place a + on one card and a − on another card. Place the integers facedown. Place the signs faceup. Each player draws a number and lays it faceup. The first player to put his or her hand over the sign of the sum of the two cards gets one point. The player with the most points wins.

Remember: Place the correct sign, either negative or positive, in your final answer.

Rational numbers include whole numbers, mixed numerals, repeating decimals, and terminating decimals.

Adding Two Positive Rational Numbers

To add two positive rational numbers follow these steps:

1. Add the two rational numbers.
2. Write the sign of the numbers in the answer.

Add $\dfrac{+2}{4} + \dfrac{+1}{4}$

Step 1: Add the rational numbers.

$$\dfrac{2}{4} + \dfrac{1}{4} = \dfrac{3}{4}$$

Step 2: Write the sign of the rational numbers in the answer.

$$\dfrac{+2}{4} + \dfrac{+1}{4} = \dfrac{+3}{4}$$

Adding Two Negative Rational Numbers

To add two negative rational numbers follow the same steps:

1. Add the two rational numbers.
2. Write the sign of the numbers in the answer.

Add $\dfrac{-3}{8} + \dfrac{-4}{8}$

Step 1: Add the rational numbers.

$$\dfrac{3}{8} + \dfrac{4}{8} = \dfrac{7}{8}$$

Step 2: Write the sign of the rational numbers in the answer.

$$\dfrac{-3}{8} + \dfrac{-4}{8} = \dfrac{-7}{8}$$

rational numbers — The set of numbers that includes fractional numbers and their opposites. Zero is also a rational number.

Adding Two Unlike Rational Numbers

To add two unlike rational numbers:

1. Subtract the two rational numbers.
2. Write the answer using the sign of the rational number that has the greater absolute value.

Add $^+2.5 + {}^-2.0$

Step 1: Subtract the two rational numbers. $\qquad 2.5 - 2.0 = 0.5$

Step 2: Show the distance from 0 to $^+2.5$ and 0 to $^-2$

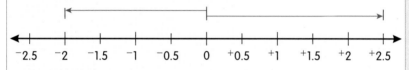

$^-2.5 \quad ^-2 \quad ^-1.5 \quad ^-1 \quad ^-0.5 \quad 0 \quad ^+0.5 \quad ^+1 \quad ^+1.5 \quad ^+2 \quad ^+2.5$

Step 3: Write the answer using the sign of the rational number with the greater absolute value. Use the sign of 2.5, because it has the greater absolute value.

$^-2$ is 2 units from 0
$^+2.5$ is 2.5 units from 0

$^+2.5 + {}^-2.0 = {}^+0.5$

$^+5.4$ $+$ $^-3.1$ $=$ $^+2.3$

unlike rational numbers — rational numbers that have different signs.

Addition Properties

There are four properties of addition: commutative property, associative property, inverse property, and zero property.

Commutative Property

The commutative property of addition allows you to add two numbers in any order you choose without affecting the sum.

Use a number line to show that $^+2 + {}^+3 = {}^+3 + {}^+2$

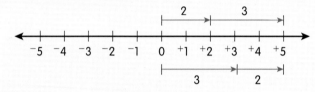

Notice, $^+2 + {}^+3 = {}^+\mathbf{5}$ and $^+3 + {}^+2 = {}^+\mathbf{5}$

In algebraic terms, with letters representing numbers, this property can be written $a + b = b + a$

Associative Property

The associative property allows you to add three or more numbers in any order you choose. The way in which you group the numbers does not affect the sum. You can use parentheses to group any two numbers.

Show that $^-1 + (^-2 + {}^-3) = (^-1 + {}^-2) + {}^-3$

Step 1: Add $^-1 + (^-2 + {}^-3)$ $^-1 + (^-2 + {}^-3)$

                                   $^-1 + \quad {}^-5 \quad = {}^-6$

Step 2: Add $(^-1 + {}^-2) + {}^-3$ $(^-1 + {}^-2) + {}^-3$

                                        $^-3 + {}^-3 \quad = {}^-6$

The property can be written $a + (b + c) = (a + b) + c$

commute—to change places.
associate—to hang out in groups.

Inverse Property

The inverse property shows that the sum of any pair of opposites is equal to zero. You can find the sum of a pair of opposites by using a number line.

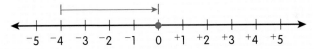

Add ⁻4 + ⁺4

Step 1: Start at ⁻4 and move four units in the positive direction (to the right).

The sum of ⁻4 + ⁺4 is 0. The sum of any pair of opposites is always zero.

In algebraic terms, $^+a + {}^-a = 0$

Zero Property

The zero property of addition shows you that the sum of zero and any other integer is always that integer.

For example: $0 + {}^-7 = {}^-7$ or $^+8 + 0 = {}^+8$ or $a + 0 = a$

Let's sum up the addition properties.

1. Commutative Property $\quad a + b = b + a$
2. Associative Property $\quad a + (b + c) = (a + b) + c$
3. Inverse Property $\quad {}^+a + {}^-a = 0$
4. Zero Property $\quad a + 0 = a$

The properties of addition can be written with letters. The letters are also known as **variables**.

a, b, and c are variables.

Like integers are integers with the same sign. You can subtract integers by adding the subtrahend's opposite or by using a number line.

Subtracting Positive Integers

To subtract an integer, add its opposite.

Subtract 7 − 9 by adding its opposite.

Step 1: Write the first number.   7

Step 2: Change the subtraction   7 +
symbol to addition.

Step 3: Write the opposite of the   7 + $^-9$ = $^-2$
second number. Add.

Subtracting $^+9$ is the same as adding $^-9$

Subtract 7 − 9 using a number line.

Step 1: Start at the first number, 7

Step 2: Using the opposite of the second number, $^-9$, move nine
places in the negative direction (to the left).

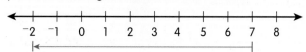

Remember: To subtract an integer, add its opposite.

In algebraic terms, $a - b = a + {}^-b$

If a number is not written with a sign, it is understood to be positive.

Subtracting Negative Integers

You can use a number line to subtract negative integers.

Subtract ⁻4 − ⁻3 using a number line.

Step 1: Locate the first integer on the number line: ⁻4

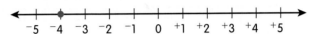

Step 2: Locate the second integer on the number line: ⁻3

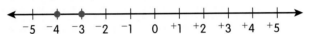

Step 3: Draw an arrow from the second integer to the first integer.

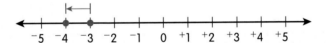

Step 4: Count the number of units you are moving and notice the direction of the arrow. One unit to the right will stand for a positive one (⁺1). One unit to the left will stand for a negative one (⁻1). You are moving one unit to the left.

Therefore, ⁻4 − ⁻3 = ⁻1

Practice subtracting integers with like signs. Use a number line to subtract integers. Check your answer by adding the opposite of the number to be subtracted to the first integer.

For all numbers a and b,
$$a - b = a + (⁻b)$$
Remember: To subtract a number, add its opposite.

People subtract integers with unlike signs when they overdraw their checking accounts. Suppose you have ⁻2 dollars in your checking account and you have to write a check for another 5 dollars. (Don't worry: You have a paycheck from your paper route to deposit in the bank by the end of the day!)

Subtracting Integers with Unlike Signs Using a Number Line

Subtract ⁻2 − 5

Step 1: Locate the first integer on the number line: ⁻2

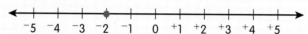

Step 2: Locate the second integer on the number line: 5

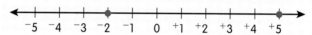

Step 3: Draw an arrow from the second integer to the first integer.

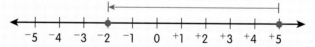

Step 4: Count the number of units you are moving and notice the direction of the arrow. You are moving 7 units to the left. This is written as ⁻7

So, ⁻2 − 5 = ⁻7

You do not have to use a number line to solve this problem.

$$^-2 - 5 = {}^-2 + {}^-5 = {}^-7$$

To subtract unlike integers without a number line, follow these steps:

1. Write the first integer.
2. Change the subtraction symbol to addition.
3. Change the sign of the second integer.

Subtract ⁻2 − 5

Step 1: Write the first integer.   ⁻2

Step 2: Change the subtraction symbol to addition.   ⁻2 +

Step 3: Change the sign of the second integer.   opposite of ⁺5 = ⁻5

Step 4: Add.   ⁻2 + ⁻5 = ⁻7

Just as on the previous page, ⁻2 − 5 = ⁻7

In algebraic terms, ⁻a − b = ⁻a + ⁻b

That's cool.

Minute Subtraction Word Game

Work with a family member. While your family member times you, decode the following word in one minute.

KEY:

⁻6 − ⁺1 = R	9 − ⁻8 = L	⁻4 − ⁺2 = E
5 − ⁻6 = A	3 − ⁺7 = G	2 − ⁻10 = B

11   17   ⁻4   ⁻6   12   ⁻7   11

—   —   —   —   —   —   —

Make up your own minute subtraction word game.

Suppose the balance in your checking account at the bank is ⁻2.50 dollars. This means that you wrote a check for more money than you had in your account. How much would you have to deposit into your savings account to make your new balance $1.50?

Use a number line to find ⁻2.50 + ? = 1.50

Step 1: Place ⁻2.50 on the number line.

Step 2: Place 1.50 on the number line.

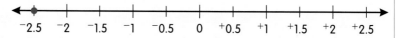

Step 3: Count the number of whole number units from ⁻2.50 to ⁺1.50

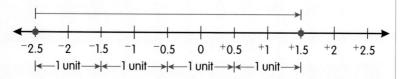

You are moving four units to the right. You need to deposit $4.00 to bring your balance to $1.50

A **rational number** can always be written as a decimal that either terminates or repeats.

To subtract rational numbers, follow these steps:

1. Write the first rational number.
2. Change the subtraction symbol to addition.
3. Change the sign of the second rational number.

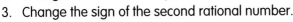

Subtract $^{+}\frac{1}{4} - {}^{+}\frac{3}{4}$

Step 1: Write the first rational number. $\qquad ^{+}\frac{1}{4}$

Step 2: Change the subtraction symbol to addition. $\qquad ^{+}\frac{1}{4} +$

Step 3: Change the sign of the second rational number. $\qquad$ opposite of $^{+}\frac{3}{4}$ is $^{-}\frac{3}{4}$

Step 4: Add. $\qquad ^{+}\frac{1}{4} + {}^{-}\frac{3}{4} = \frac{1 + (^{-}3)}{4} = \frac{^{-}2}{4}$

Step 5: Reduce the fraction. $\qquad \frac{^{-}2}{4} = \frac{^{-}1}{2}$

Therefore, $^{+}\frac{1}{4} - {}^{+}\frac{3}{4} = \frac{^{-}1}{2}$

I get it!

To **reduce a fraction,** divide each term by the greatest common factor.

$$\frac{2 \div 2}{4 \div 2} = \frac{1}{2}$$

You can think of multiplication as repeated addition.

What is ⁻6 added to itself 3 times?   ⁻6 + ⁻6 + ⁻6 = ⁻18

Instead of adding you can use multiplication to solve this problem.

$$3 \times {}^-6 = {}^-18$$

The integers you are multiplying are called factors, and the answer is called the product. In the above example 3 and ⁻6 are factors and ⁻18 is the product.

Multiplying Like Integers

Like integers are integers with the same sign. When two factors have the same sign, the product is positive.

    1. positive × positive = positive $^+a \times {}^+b = {}^+ab$

    2. negative × negative = positive $^-a \times {}^-b = {}^+ab$

Multiply ⁺4 × ⁺8

Step 1: Multiply as whole numbers.   4 × 8 = 32

Step 2: Place the sign.   ⁺4 × ⁺8 = ⁺32
         positive × positive = positive

You can write a positive integer with or without the positive sign.

         ⁺4 × ⁺8 = ⁺32,   or   4 × 8 = 32

Multiply ⁻6 × ⁻9

Step 1: Multiply as whole numbers.   6 × 9 = 54

Step 2: Place the sign.   ⁻6 × ⁻9 = ⁺54
         negative × negative = positive
      ⁻6 × ⁻9 = ⁺54   or   ⁻6 × ⁻9 = 54

Determine the sign of the product after each pair.

        (⁻1 × ⁻1) × ⁻1 × ⁻1 =

          ⁺1 × ⁻1   × ⁻1 =

            ⁻1   × ⁻1 = ⁺1

Multiplying Unlike Integers

Unlike integers are integers that have different signs. When two factors have different signs, the product is negative.

1. positive $\times$ negative = negative $a \times {}^-b = {}^-ab$
2. negative $\times$ positive = negative ${}^-a \times b = {}^-ab$

Multiply $^-7 \times {}^+3$

Step 1: Multiply as whole numbers. $7 \times 3 = 21$

Step 2: Place the sign. $^-7 \times {}^+3 = {}^-21$
       negative $\times$ positive = negative

Multiply $^+5 \times {}^-3$

Step 1: Multiply as whole numbers. $5 \times 3 = 15$

Step 2: Place the sign. $^+5 \times {}^-3 = {}^-15$
       positive $\times$ negative = negative

Multiplying Integers

Factor	$\times$	Factor	=	Product
positive	$\times$	positive	=	positive
negative	$\times$	negative	=	positive
negative	$\times$	positive	=	negative
positive	$\times$	negative	=	negative

I can remember this!

If the factors in a multiplication problem have the same signs, the sign of the answer is **positive.** If they have different signs, the answer is **negative.**

29

13 Multiplying Signed Rational Numbers

Signed rational numbers are positive and negative rational numbers, such as $^+\frac{1}{2}$, $^-0.7$, $^+\frac{1}{9}$, and $^-4.6$

Suppose you wanted to multiply two or more signed rational numbers. How does the sign of the product change?

Multiplying Like Rational Numbers

Like rational numbers have the same sign. Remember, when two factors have the same sign, the product is positive.

Multiply $\frac{^-1}{2} \times \frac{^-3}{4}$

Step 1: Multiply as fractions.

$$\frac{1}{2} \times \frac{3}{4} = \frac{1 \times 3}{2 \times 4} = \frac{3}{8}$$

Step 2: Place the sign in the answer.

negative $\times$ negative = positive

$$\frac{^-1}{2} \times \frac{^-3}{4} = \frac{^+3}{8}$$

Multiplying Unlike Rational Numbers

Unlike rational numbers have different signs. Remember, when two factors have different signs, the product is negative.

Multiply $^-0.1 \times {}^+0.3$

Step 1: Multiply as decimals.

0.1	**1 decimal place**
$\times$ 0.3	**1 decimal place**
0.03	**2 decimal places**

Step 2: Place the sign.

$^-0.1 \times {}^+0.3 = {}^-0.03$

Multiplying rational numbers follows the same rules as multiplying integers.

negative $\times$ negative = positive   negative $\times$ positive = negative

positive $\times$ positive = positive   positive $\times$ negative = negative

Multiplying Two or More Signed Rational Numbers

If all the factors are positive, the product is positive.

2 positives	$^{+}a \times {}^{+}b = {}^{+}ab$
3 positives	$^{+}a \times {}^{+}b \times {}^{+}c = {}^{+}abc$
4 positives	$^{+}a \times {}^{+}b \times {}^{+}c \times {}^{+}d = {}^{+}abcd$

Examples:

$$^{+}6 \times {}^{+}8 = {}^{+}48$$
$$^{+}3 \times {}^{+}3 \times {}^{+}2 = {}^{+}18$$

If there is an odd number of negative factors, the product is negative.

1 negative	$^{+}a \times {}^{-}b = {}^{-}ab$
3 negatives	$^{-}a \times {}^{-}b \times {}^{-}c = {}^{-}abc$
3 negatives and 1 positive	$^{-}a \times {}^{-}b \times {}^{-}c \times {}^{+}d = {}^{-}abcd$

Examples:

$$^{+}2 \times \frac{^{-}2}{3} = \frac{^{-}4}{3}$$
$$^{-}4 \times {}^{-}6 \times {}^{-}2 = {}^{-}48$$

If there is an even number of negative factors, the product is positive.

2 negatives	$^{-}a \times {}^{-}b = {}^{+}ab$
2 negatives and 1 positive	$^{-}a \times {}^{-}b \times {}^{+}c = {}^{+}abc$
4 negatives	$^{-}a \times {}^{-}b \times {}^{-}c \times {}^{-}d = {}^{+}abcd$

Examples:

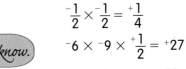
That's good to know.

$$\frac{^{-}1}{2} \times \frac{^{-}1}{2} = \frac{^{+}1}{4}$$
$$^{-}6 \times {}^{-}9 \times \frac{^{+}1}{2} = {}^{+}27$$
$$^{-}3 \times {}^{-}1 \times {}^{-}5 \times {}^{-}10 = {}^{+}150$$

When doing multiplication problems, remember to assign the correct sign to the answer.

Commutative Property

You can multiply two integers in any order you choose without affecting the answer.

Prove whether the equation $^+a \times {}^-b = {}^-b \times {}^+a$ is true.

Multiply the left side of the equation. $^+a \times {}^-b$

Step 1: Multiply as whole numbers. $a \times b = ab$

Step 2: Place the sign. $^+a \times {}^-b = {}^-ab$
positive $\times$ negative = negative

Multiply the right side of the equation. $^-b \times {}^+a$

Step 1: Multiply as whole numbers. $b \times a = ba$

Step 2: Place the sign. $^-b \times {}^+a = {}^-ba$
negative $\times$ positive = negative

Notice that the answers are the same: $^-ab = {}^-ba$
So, $^+a \times {}^-b = {}^-b \times {}^+a$

For example: $^+8 \times {}^-4 = {}^-4 \times {}^+8$
$^-32 = {}^-32$

Identity Property

When you multiply 1 and any other number, the answer is always that number ($1 \times a = a$). For example: $1 \times {}^-5 = {}^-5$

Zero Property

When you multiply zero and any other number, the answer is always zero ($0 \times a = 0$). For example: $0 \times {}^-9 = 0$

---

commutative property: $^+a \times {}^-b = {}^-b \times {}^+a$
identity property: $1 \times a = a$
zero property: $0 \times a = 0$

Associative Property

You can multiply three or more integers in any order you choose without affecting the answer.

Prove whether the equation
$^+2 \times (^-4 \times {}^-3) = (^+2 \times {}^-4) \times {}^-3$ **is true.**

Step 1: Multiply the left side of the equation.

$^+2 \times (^-4 \times {}^-3)$

$^+2 \times {}^+12 \quad = {}^+\mathbf{24}$

Step 2: Multiply the right side of the equation.

$(^+2 \times {}^-4) \times {}^-3$

$^-8 \times {}^-3 = {}^+\mathbf{24}$

The products are the same. Therefore multiplication is associative.

Distributive Property of Multiplication over Addition

The distributive property of multiplication over addition uses multiplication and addition. So, you can separate a multiplication problem into two problems.

$$^-2 \times (^+7 + {}^-6) = (^-2 \times {}^+7) + (^-2 \times {}^-6)$$

The $^-2$ was **distributed** to both addends, $^+7$ and $^-6$.

$$^-2 \times (^+7 + {}^-6) = (^-2 \times {}^+7) + (^-2 \times {}^-6)$$

$$^-2 \times {}^+1 \quad = \quad {}^-14 \quad + \quad {}^+12$$

$$^-2 \quad = \quad {}^-2$$

The answers are the same on both sides of the equation.

For any numbers, $a \times (b + c) = (a \times b) + (a \times c)$

associative property: $a \times (b \times c) = (a \times b) \times c$
distributive property of multiplication over addition:
$a \times (b + c) = (a \times b) + (a \times c)$

The terms associated with division are *dividend*, *divisor*, and *quotient*.

$12 \div 3 = 4$

$$\text{dividend} \div \text{divisor} = \text{quotient}$$

Divide integers just like whole numbers.

If both integers are positive, the answer is positive.

$$^+a \div {^+b} = \frac{^+a}{b}$$

If both integers are negative, the answer is positive.

$$^-a \div {^-b} = \frac{^+a}{b}$$

If one integer is positive and one is negative, the answer will be negative.

$$^+a \div {^-b} = \frac{^-a}{b}$$

Dividing Like Integers

Divide $^+56 \div {^+8}$

Step 1: Divide as whole numbers. $56 \div 8 = 7$

Step 2: Place the sign. $^+56 \div {^+8} = {^+7}$
positive ÷ positive = positive

Divide $^-35 \div {^-7}$

Step 1: Divide as whole numbers. $35 \div 7 = 5$

Step 2: Place the sign. $^-35 \div {^-7} = {^+5}$
negative ÷ negative = positive

The quotient of two numbers with like signs is always positive.
The quotient of two numbers with unlike signs is always negative.

Dividing Unlike Integers

When you divide a negative integer and a positive integer, the answer will be negative.

Divide $^+24 \div {}^-4$

Step 1: Divide as whole numbers.

$24 \div 4 = 6$

Step 2: Place the sign.
positive ÷ negative = negative

$^+24 \div {}^-4 = {}^-6$

Remember:

Sign of the two integers		Sign of the answer	
2 positive	$(^+a \div {}^+b)$	positive	$(\frac{^+a}{b})$
2 negative	$(^-a \div {}^-b)$	positive	$(\frac{^+a}{b})$
1 positive, 1 negative	$(^+a \div {}^-b)$	negative	$(\frac{^-a}{b})$

If you divide or multiply integers with the same sign, the answer will be positive.
If you divide or multiply integers with different signs, the answer will be negative.

$$24 \div 4 = 6 \qquad\qquad 24 \div {}^-4 = {}^-6$$
$$4 \times 4 = 16 \qquad\qquad 4 \times {}^-4 = {}^-16$$

Just like with multiplication, if there is an even number of negative numbers in the division problem, the answer will be positive. If there is an odd number of negative numbers, the answer will be negative.

To divide signed rational numbers, first divide the numbers, ignoring their signs. Then place the sign in the answer.

Dividing Like Rational Numbers

Divide $\dfrac{^-1}{2} \div \dfrac{^-1}{4}$

Step 1: Divide as rational numbers.

$$\frac{1}{2} \div \frac{1}{4} = \frac{1}{2} \times \frac{4}{1} = \frac{4}{2} = 2$$

Step 2: Place the sign.

$$\frac{^-1}{2} \div \frac{^-1}{4} = {}^+2$$

Divide $^-0.50 \div {}^-0.25$

Step 1: Divide as rational numbers

$$0.25\overline{)0.50}^{\,2}$$

Step 2: Place the sign.

$$^-0.50 \div {}^-0.25 = {}^+2$$

Divide $^+0.50 \div {}^+0.25$

Step 1: Divide as rational numbers.

$$0.25\overline{)0.50} \qquad 25\overline{)50}^{\,2}$$
$$\underline{-50}$$
$$0$$

Step 2: Place the sign.

$$^+0.50 \div {}^+0.25 = {}^+2$$

Divide $\dfrac{^+1}{2} \div \dfrac{^+1}{4}$

Step 1: Divide as rational numbers.

$$\frac{1}{2} \div \frac{1}{4} = \frac{1}{2} \times \frac{4}{1} = \frac{4}{2} = 2$$

Step 2: Place the sign.

$$\frac{^+1}{2} \div \frac{^+1}{4} = {}^+2$$

If all the rational numbers in a division problem are positive, then the answer will be positive.

Dividing Unlike Rational Numbers

Divide $\dfrac{^+1}{3} \div \dfrac{^-1}{9}$

Step 1: Divide as rational numbers.

$$\frac{1}{3} \div \frac{1}{9} = \frac{1}{3} \times \frac{9}{1} = \frac{9}{3} = 3$$

Step 2: Place the sign.
positive ÷ negative = negative

$$\frac{^+1}{3} \div \frac{^-1}{9} = {}^-3$$

Here's a summary of division of rational numbers.

1. If both rational numbers are positive, the answer will be positive.
2. If both rational numbers are negative, the answer will be positive.
3. If there is a negative integer and a positive integer, the answer will be negative.

Take Stock

The stock exchange uses rational numbers to report gains and losses. Look in the business section of your newspaper to find your favorite name-brand game or clothing. Record the closing cost of that company's stock for 5 days. Find the average by adding the closing cost and dividing the sum by 5.

When you divide a negative integer and a positive integer, the answer will be negative.

Numbers, variables, and operation signs are used to write algebraic expressions. Some examples of algebraic expressions are:

$$3d \qquad a - 14 \qquad 4x + 3 \qquad \frac{x}{10}$$

Word Expressions

Algebraic expressions can be used to replace word expressions. The following is a list of key words used in algebraic expressions:

Key words	Operation
more than, increased by, sum	addition ($+$)
less than, decreased by, difference	subtraction ($-$)
times, product	multiplication ($\times$)
divided by, quotient	division ($\div$)

Write an algebraic expression for: 3 times the distance you walk to school.

Step 1: Select a letter to represent the unknown. $\quad d =$ distance walked to school

Step 2: Identify the operation. $\quad$ *times* means "to multiply"

Step 3: Write the algebraic expression. $\quad 3d$

$3d$ means to multiply 3 times d. You do not have to write the multiplication sign.

variables—Letters such as a, x, and y that are used in mathematical expressions to stand for names.

Evaluating Expressions

You can find the value of an algebraic expression by replacing the variables with numbers.

Find the value of $6a + 12$ when $a = 5$

Step 1: Write the expression. $6a + 12$

Step 2: Replace the variable for $6(5) + 12$
the given value.

Step 3: Perform the operation. Always do multiplication before addition when both exist in an equation, unless parentheses tell you otherwise.

$$6(5) + 12$$
$$30 + 12 = 42$$

The value of $6a + 12$ when $a = 5$ is 42

Find the value of $\frac{x}{8} - 3$ when $x = 40$

Step 1: Write the expression. $\frac{x}{8} - 3$

Step 2: Replace the variable for $\frac{40}{8} - 3$
the given value.

Step 3: Perform the operation. $\frac{40}{8} - 3$
$$5 - 3 = 2$$

The value of $\frac{x}{8} - 3$ when $x = 40$ is 2

The letters of the alphabet are used to represent variables. They can be used with other letters or with numbers to create expressions or sentences.

expression—A collection of numbers, symbols, and letters with no equal sign, such as $6a + 12$.

equation—Statement that does have an equal sign, such as $6a + 12 = 24$.

An algebraic sentence is a mathematical sentence that contains at least one variable and one of the following symbols:

Symbol	Meaning
$=$	is equal to
$<$	is less than
$>$	is greater than
$\geq$	is greater than or equal to
$\leq$	is less than or equal to

Word Sentences

Algebraic sentences are used to represent word sentences.

Write an algebraic sentence for the following word sentence: The height of the cherry tree is greater than 9 meters.

Step 1: Select any letter in the alphabet to represent the variable (the height of the tree). c = height of the cherry tree

Step 2: Identify the symbol.   is greater than: $>$

Step 3: Write the algebraic sentence. $c > 9$

Write an algebraic sentence for the following word sentence: The sum of two numbers is 26.

Step 1: Select any two letters to represent the two variables. x = one variable
y = other variable

Step 2: Identify the symbol and operation.   *is* means "$=$"
operation: $+$ (for sum)

Step 3: Write the algebraic sentence. $x + y = 26$

When both multiplication and addition are in an equation, always do the **multiplication first** (unless parentheses tell you otherwise).

Evaluating Algebraic Sentences

You can tell whether an algebraic sentence is true or false for any given number.

Evaluate $4x - 3 = 17$ when x is 5

Step 1: Write the algebraic sentence. $4x - 3 = 17$

Step 2: Replace the value for x. $4(5) - 3 = 17$

Step 3: Perform the operation. $4(5) - 3 = 17$
$$20 - 3 = 17$$
$$17 = 17$$

The number on the left side of the equation is equal to the number on the right side of the equation. The algebraic sentence $4x - 3 = 17$ is true for the value of x.

The value for x is the *solution* for the algebraic sentence.

Evaluate $6x = 4y + 3$ when $x = 3$ and $y = 2$

Step 1: Write the algebraic sentence. $6x = 4y + 3$

Step 2: Replace the value for x and y. $6(3) = 4(2) + 3$

Step 3: Perform the operation. $6(3) = 4(2) + 3$
$$18 = 8 + 3$$
$$18 \neq 11$$

The number on the left side of the equation does not equal the number on the right side of the equation. The values for x and y are not solutions for the algebraic sentence.

solution — The set of numbers which, when used instead of letters, make the algebraic sentence true.
The solution for $5 + x = 7$ is $x = 2$ since $5 + 2 = 7$

Variables are used in algebra to take the place of names.

$$3a + 5 \qquad a \text{ is a variable.}$$

It may stand for the number of apples on a tree or the number of people in a class.

Adding and Subtracting with Variables

You can only add or subtract values that have the same variable.

$$3a + 2a = 5a$$
$$5x + 2x = 7x$$
$$\frac{3}{4}c - \frac{2}{4}c = \frac{1}{4}c$$

You cannot add or subtract values that do not have the same variables.

$$3a + 5b$$
$$\frac{^-1}{6}x + 2y$$
$$15m - 0.6x$$

To add variables, add the numbers in front of the letters.

$$3a + 2a = 5a$$
$$5q + {}^-1.5q = 3.5q$$

A variable without a number in front of it is the same as a variable with the number 1 in front of it.

$$3a + a = 3a + 1a = 4a$$

To subtract variables, subtract the numbers in front of the letters.

$$3a - 2a = a$$
$$16x - \frac{1}{2}x = 15\frac{1}{2}x$$

A variable without a number in front of it is the same as a variable with the number 1 in front of it.

$$a = 1a$$

Order of Operation

In algebra, parentheses are often used to show you which operation to do first.

Solve the expression 3 (4 + 6)

Step 1: The parentheses show that you should first do addition.

$4 + 6 = 10$

Step 2: Multiply the answer by 3.

$3 (10) = 30$

So, $3 (4 + 6) = 30$

Sometimes a problem is written without parentheses:

$$2 \times 4 + 3$$

Although you can do the problem two ways, only one way is correct.

Right
$2 \times 4 + 3$
$8 + 3 = 11$

Wrong
$2 \times 4 + 3$
$2 \times 7 = 14$

Perform operations in this order:

1. Perform all operations inside parentheses.
2. Do all multiplication or division.
3. Do all addition or subtraction.

Always perform operations with multiplication and division from left to right.

Equations are algebraic sentences that show an equal relationship (=) between two expressions.

$$x - 20 = 36 \text{ is an equation.}$$

To solve an equation for an unknown means to find a solution, or a value, for the unknown variable.

When solving an equation, you need to get the variable by itself on one side of the equation. To do this, use the inverse operation. If the equation uses subtraction, solve the equation by using addition. If the equation uses addition, use subtraction to solve it.

Solve $x - 20 = 36$

$x - 20 = 36$ **Step 1:** Write the equation.

$$\begin{aligned} x - 20 &= 36 \\ +20 &= +20 \end{aligned}$$

Step 2: Use addition to get the variable, x, by itself on one side of the equation. Add the same number to both sides of the equation.

$$\begin{aligned} x - \cancel{20} &= 36 \\ \cancel{+20} &= +20 \\ x &= 56 \end{aligned}$$

Step 3: Perform the operation.

Step 4: Write the solution.

$$x = 56$$

Check the solution.

$x - 20 = 36$ **Step 1:** Write the equation.

$56 - 20 = 36$ **Step 2:** Replace the variable with the solution in the equation.

To **check your solution**, replace the variable with the solution. Then, see whether the equation is true.

Step 3: Perform the operation.

$$56 - 20 = 36$$
$$36 = 36$$

The equation is true because $36 = 36$. Therefore, 56 is the solution for x in the equation $x - 20 = 36$

Solving Subtraction Equations with Signed Numbers

Solve: $x - {}^-40 = 50$

$x - {}^-40 = 50$

Step 1: Write the equation.

$\begin{aligned} x - {}^-40 &= 50 \\ + {}^-40 &= + {}^-40 \end{aligned}$

Step 2: Use addition to solve the equation. Add the same number to both sides of the equation.

$\begin{aligned} x - 40 &= 50 \\ +40 &= + {}^-40 \\ \hline x &= 10 \end{aligned}$

$x = 10$

Step 3: Perform the operation.

Step 4: Write the solution.

Check the solution.

$x - {}^-40 = 50$

Step 1: Write the equation.

$10 - {}^-40 = 50$

Step 2: Replace the variable with the solution in the equation.

$\begin{aligned} 10 - {}^-40 &= 50 \\ 10 + {}^+40 &= 50 \\ 50 &= 50 \end{aligned}$

Step 3: Perform the operation. Change the subtraction symbol to addition. Change the sign of ${}^-40$. Add.

The equation is true because $50 = 50$. Therefore, 10 is the solution for x in the equation $x - {}^-40 = 50$

operation — A way of combining numbers. The most common operation combines two numbers, such as $4 \times 2 = 8$ or $10 - {}^-40 = 50$.

21 Solving Equations Using Subtraction

Subtraction is used to solve equations that show addition.

The following equations show addition:

$$x + 9 = 20 \qquad x + 3 = {}^-5$$

Remember, you need to get the variable by itself on one side of the equation. To do this you have to use the inverse operation. The inverse operation of addition is subtraction. If the equation shows addition, use subtraction to solve it.

Solve $x + 9 = 20$

Step 1: Write the equation.

$$x + 9 = 20$$

Step 2: Use subtraction to solve the equation. Subtract 9 from both sides of the equation.

$$\begin{aligned} x + 9 &= 20 \\ -9 & \quad -9 \end{aligned}$$

Step 3: Perform the operation.

Step 4: Write the solution.

$$\begin{aligned} x + 9 &= 20 \\ -9 & \quad -9 \\ x &= 11 \end{aligned}$$

$$x = 11$$

Check the solution.

Step 1: Write the equation.

$$x + 9 = 20$$

Step 2: Replace the variable with the solution in the equation.

$$11 + 9 = 20$$

Step 3: Perform the operation.

$$11 + 9 = 20$$
$$20 = 20$$

The equation is true because $20 = 20$. Therefore, 11 is the solution for x in the equation $x + 9 = 20$.

When the equation is true, you have calculated the correct solution.

Solving Addition Equations with Signed Numbers

Solve $x + {}^-6 = {}^-5$

Step 1: Write the equation.

$$x + {}^-6 = {}^-5$$

Step 2: Use subtraction to solve the equation. Subtract the same number from both sides of the equation.

$$\begin{array}{rcr} x + {}^-6 &=& {}^-5 \\ -{}^-6 &=& -{}^-6 \end{array}$$

Step 3: Perform the operation. Change the minus sign to a plus sign. Change the sign of ${}^-6$. Add. $({}^-5 - {}^-6 = {}^-5 + {}^+6 = 1)$

$$\begin{array}{rcr} x + {}^-6 &=& {}^-5 \\ -{}^-6 &=& -{}^-6 \\ x &=& 1 \end{array}$$

Step 4: Write the solution.

$$x = 1$$

Check the solution.

Step 1: Write the equation.

$$x + {}^-6 = {}^-5$$

Step 2: Replace the variable with the solution in the equation.

$$1 + {}^-6 = {}^-5$$

Step 3: Perform the operation.

$$\begin{array}{rcl} 1 + {}^-6 &=& {}^-5 \\ {}^-5 &=& {}^-5 \end{array}$$

The equation is true because ${}^-5 = {}^-5$. Therefore, 1 is the solution for x in the equation $x + {}^-6 = {}^-5$.

Make up your own addition equations and solve them using subtraction.

inverse operations:
Addition is the inverse of subtraction.
Multiplication is the inverse of division.

22 Solving Equations Using Multiplication

Multiplication and division are inverse operations. Multiplication undoes division. The following equation shows division:

$$\frac{x}{4} = 7$$

This equation is read, "A number divided by 4 is 7."

To solve for the variable (x), find the number that the variable is divided by, and then multiply both sides of the equation by that number. This will get the variable by itself.

Solve $\frac{x}{4} = 7$

Step 1: Write the equation. $\frac{x}{4} = 7$

Step 2: Multiply both sides of the equation by 4. $4 \times \frac{x}{4} = 7 \times 4$

Step 3: Perform the operation. $\frac{4}{1} \times \frac{x}{4} = 7 \times 4$

Step 4: Write the solution. $x = 28$

Check the solution.

Step 1: Write the equation. $\frac{x}{4} = 7$

Step 2: Replace the variable with the solution in the equation. $\frac{28}{4} = 7$

Step 3: Perform the operation. $\frac{28}{4} = 7$
$7 = 7$

The equation is true because $7 = 7$. Therefore, 28 is the solution for x in the equation $\frac{x}{4} = 7$.

Remember: To solve an algebraic equation, you need to get the variable on one side of the equation by itself.

Solving Division Equations with Signed Numbers

Solve $\frac{x}{3} = {}^-8$

Step 1: Write the equation.

$$\frac{x}{3} = {}^-8$$

Step 2: Multiply both sides of the equation by 3.

$$3 \times \frac{x}{3} = {}^-8 \times 3$$

Step 3: Perform the operation. negative × positive = negative

$$\cancel{3} \times \frac{x}{\cancel{3}} = {}^-8 \times 3$$

Step 4: Write the solution.

$$x = {}^-24$$

Check the solution.

Step 1: Write the equation.

$$\frac{x}{3} = {}^-8$$

Step 2: Replace the variable with the solution in the equation.

$$\frac{{}^-24}{3} = {}^-8$$

Step 3: Perform the operation.

$$\frac{{}^-24}{3} = {}^-8$$
$${}^-8 = {}^-8$$

The equation is true because ${}^-8 = {}^-8$. Therefore, ${}^-24$ is the solution for x in the equation $\frac{x}{3} = {}^-8$.

I can multiply both sides by the reciprocal. The reciprocal of $\frac{1}{3}$ is $\frac{3}{1}$

If both sides of an equation are multiplied by the same number, the solution does not change.

You can use division to solve multiplication equations.

An example of a multiplication equation is $6n = 42$.
This equation is read, "6 times a number is 42."

In this equation, 6 is called the coefficient and n is the variable (n). To solve a multiplication equation, find the number that the variable is multiplied by and then divide both sides of the equation by that number. This will get the variable by itself.

Solve $6n = 42$

Step 1: Write the equation. $\qquad\qquad\qquad\qquad 6n = 42$

Step 2: Divide both sides of the equation by 6. $\qquad\qquad \dfrac{6n}{6} = \dfrac{42}{6}$

Step 3: Perform the operation. $\qquad\qquad\qquad \dfrac{\cancel{6}n}{\cancel{6}} = \dfrac{\cancel{42}^{7}}{\cancel{6}}$

Step 4: Write the solution. $\qquad\qquad\qquad\qquad n = 7$

Check the solution.

Step 1: Write the equation. $\qquad\qquad\qquad\qquad 6n = 42$

Step 2: Replace the value of the solution in the equation. $\qquad 6 \times 7 = 42$

Step 3: Perform the operation. $\qquad\qquad\qquad 6 \times 7 = 42$

$\qquad\qquad\qquad\qquad\qquad\qquad\qquad\qquad 42 = 42$

The equation is true because $42 = 42$. Therefore, 7 is the solution for n in the equation $6n = 42$.

coefficient — The number that the variable is multiplied by.

Solving Multiplication Equations with Signed Numbers

Here is how to solve a multiplication equation that contains signed numbers.

Solve $^-2n = ^-20$

Step 1: Write the equation.

$$^-2n = ^-20$$

Step 2: Divide both sides of the equation by $^-2$.

$$\frac{^-2n}{^-2} = \frac{^-20}{^-2}$$

Step 3: Perform the operation.

$$\frac{\cancel{^-2}n}{\cancel{^-2}} = \frac{\overset{10}{\cancel{^-20}}}{\cancel{^-2}}$$

$$\frac{\text{negative}}{\text{negative}} = \text{positive}$$

Step 4: Write the solution.

$$n = 10$$

Check the solution.

Step 1: Write the equation.

$$^-2n = ^-20$$

Step 2: Replace the variable with the solution in the equation.

$$^-2 \times 10 = ^-20$$

Step 3: Perform the operation.

$$^-2 \times 10 = ^-20$$
$$^-20 = ^-20$$

The equation is true because $^-20 = ^-20$. Therefore, 10 is the solution for n in the equation $^-2n = ^-20$

Practice solving multiplication equations using division. Make up your own multiplication equations.

For example: $3n = 33$ or $^-6n = ^-72$

If both sides of an equation are divided by the same number, the solution does not change.

Solving Equations with Rational Numbers

If an equation shows:

1. *Addition*: Subtract the number that the variable is being added to from both sides of the equation.
2. *Subtraction*: Add the number that is being subtracted from the variable to both sides of the equation.
3. *Multiplication*: Divide both sides of the equation by the number that the variable is being multiplied by.
4. *Division*: Multiply both sides of the equation by the number that the variable is being divided by.

Solving Addition or Subtraction Equations with Rational Numbers

Solve $x + 6.8 = {}^-4.3$

Step 1: Write the equation.
$$x + 6.8 = {}^-4.3$$

Step 2: Subtract 6.8 from both sides of the equation.
$$x + 6.8 = {}^-4.3$$
$$\underline{ - 6.8 = -6.8}$$

Step 3: Write the solution.
$$x = {}^-11.1$$

Step 4: Check the solution.
$${}^-11.1 + 6.8 = {}^-4.3$$

Solve: $x - 4.6 = {}^-10.3$

Step 1: Write the equation.
$$x - 4.6 = {}^-10.3$$

Step 2: Add 4.6 to both sides of the equation.
$$x - 4.6 = {}^-10.3$$
$$\underline{ + 4.6 = +4.6}$$

Step 3: Write the solution.
$$x = {}^-5.7$$

Step 4: Check the solution.
$${}^-5.7 - 4.6 = {}^-10.3$$

Solve equations with rational numbers just as you would with whole numbers or integers.

Solving Multiplication Equations with Rational Numbers

Solve $5.8n = {}^-23.2$

Step 1: Write the equation. $\qquad\qquad\qquad 5.8n = {}^-23.2$

Step 2: Divide both sides of the $\qquad\qquad \dfrac{5.8n}{5.8} = \dfrac{{}^-23.2}{5.8}$
equation by 5.8

Step 3: Write the solution. $\qquad\qquad\qquad\qquad n = {}^-4$

Check the solution.

Step 1: Write the equation. $\qquad\qquad\qquad 5.8n = {}^-23.2$

Step 2: Replace the variable with the $\qquad 5.8 \times {}^-4 = {}^-23.2$
solution in the equation.

Step 3: Perform the operation. $\qquad\qquad 5.8 \times {}^-4 = {}^-23.2$
$\qquad\qquad\qquad\qquad\qquad\qquad\qquad {}^-23.2 = {}^-23.2$

The equation is true because ${}^-23.2 = {}^-23.2$. Therefore, ${}^-4$ is the solution for n in the equation $5.8n = {}^-23.2$.

Solving Division Equations with Rational Numbers

Solve $\dfrac{n}{5} = 4.5$

Step 1: Write the equation. $\qquad\qquad\qquad\qquad \dfrac{n}{5} = 4.5$

Step 2: Multiply both sides of the $\qquad 5 \times \dfrac{n}{5} = 4.5 \times 5$
equation by 5.

Step 3: Write the solution. $\qquad\qquad\qquad\qquad n = 22.5$

Step 4: Check the solution. $\qquad\qquad\qquad \dfrac{22.5}{5} = 4.5$

Don't forget to check your solution.

Two-step equations involve more than one mathematical operation.

Addition and Multiplication

The following two-step equation shows addition and multiplication: $7n + 12 = 54$. This equation is read, "The sum of 7 times a number plus 12 is 54."

Solve $7n + 12 = 54$

Step 1: Write the equation.

$$7n + 12 = 54$$

Step 2: Subtract 12 from both sides of the equation.

$$\begin{aligned} 7n + 12 &= 54 \\ -12 &= -12 \\ \hline 7n &= 42 \end{aligned}$$

Step 3: Divide both sides of the equation by 7.

$$\frac{7n}{7} = \frac{42}{7}$$
$$n = 42 \div 7$$

Step 4: Write the solution.

$$n = 6$$

Step 5: Check the solution.

$$7(6) + 12 = 54$$

To solve an equation that has addition and multiplication:

1. **Subtract** from both sides of the equation the number that is being added to the variable.
2. **Divide** both sides of the equation by the number that the variable is being multiplied by.

Take it one step at a time!

Subtraction and Division

The following two-step equation shows subtraction and division:

$$\frac{x}{5} - 6 = 4$$

This equation is read, "The difference between some number divided by 5 and 6 is 4."

To solve an equation that shows subtraction and division, follow these steps:

1. **Add** to both sides of the equation the number that is being subtracted from the variable.
2. **Multiply** both sides of the equation by the number that the variable is being divided by.

Solve $\frac{n}{5} - 6 = 4$

Step 1: Write the equation.

$$\frac{n}{5} - 6 = 4$$

Step 2: Add 6 to both sides of the equation.

$$\frac{n}{5} - \cancel{6} = 4$$
$$+ \cancel{6} = +6$$
$$\frac{n}{5} = 10$$

Step 3: Multiply both sides of the equation by 5.

$$5 \times \frac{n}{5} = 10 \times 5$$
$$\cancel{5} \times \frac{n}{\cancel{5}} = 10 \times 5$$

Step 4: Write the solution.

$$n = 50$$

Step 5: Check the solution.

$$\frac{50}{5} - 6 = 4$$

Make up two-step equations using multiplication and addition or division and subtraction. Solve each equation with a friend.

Multistep equations have equations with two or more operations.

Solve $\frac{2n}{3} + 7 = 25$

Step 1: Write the equation.

$$\frac{2n}{3} + 7 = 25$$

Step 2: Subtract 7 from both sides of the equation.

$$\frac{2n}{3} + 7 - 7 = 25 - 7$$
$$\frac{2n}{3} = 18$$

Step 3: Multiply both sides of the equation by 3.

$$3 \times \frac{2n}{3} = 18 \times 3$$
$$2n = 54$$

Step 4: Divide both sides of the equation by 2.

$$\frac{2n}{2} = \frac{54}{2}$$

Step 5: Write the solution.

$$n = 27$$

Check the solution.

Step 1: Write the equation.

$$\frac{2n}{3} + 7 = 25$$

Step 2: Replace the variable with the solution in the equation and simplify.

$$\frac{2(27)}{3} + 7 = 25$$
$$\frac{54}{3} + 7 = 25$$
$$18 + 7 = 25$$
$$25 = 25$$

The equation is true because $25 = 25$. Therefore, 27 is the solution for n in the equation $\frac{2n}{3} + 7 = 25$.

The goal in solving two-step equations is to get the variable all by itself. To solve for the variable, do the addition or subtraction **first** and do multiplication or division **last**.

Problem Solving Using Multistep Equations

You want to buy a bike for $90. You already have $20. If you earn $5 per hour delivering newspapers, how many hours must you work to earn the rest of the money you need to buy the bike?

Step 1: What information do you know and what must you find?

know: need $90
have $20
earn $5 per hour

Step 2: Write an algebraic equation. Let n = number of hours.

$$5n + 20 = 90$$
earn + have = need

Step 3: Subtract 20 from both sides of the equation.

$$5n + 20 - 20 = 90 - 20$$
$$5n = 70$$

Step 4: Divide both sides of the equation by 5.

$$\frac{5n}{5} = \frac{70}{5}$$

Step 5: Write the solution.

$$n = 14$$

You must work 14 hours to buy the bike for $90. Let's check our solution: 5×14 hours = $70; $20 (which is what you already have) plus $70 equals the $90 you need to buy the bike.

I can do this!

Make up problems using multistep equations. Solve each equation with a friend.

If the inequalities shown involve:

1. *Addition*: Subtract from both sides of the algebraic sentence the number that is being added to the variable.
2. *Subtraction*: Add to both sides of the algebraic sentence the number that is being subtracted from the variable.

Solving an Inequality Using Addition

Solve and graph the inequality $x - 7 < -4$

Step 1: Write the inequality.

$$x - 7 < {}^-4$$

Step 2: Add 7 to both sides of the inequality.

$$x - 7 + 7 < {}^-4 + 7$$

Step 3: Write the solution.

$$x < 3$$

Step 4: Show the solution set, $x < 3$, using a graph.

Place an open circle on the 3. This shows that 3 is the start of all numbers in the solution set, but is not included. (A solid circle would mean that 3 was included, $x \le 3$.)

Draw a dark line over the number line to show on which side of 3 lies the solution set. Notice that the arrow at the end of the graph is dark. It shows that the solution includes all numbers less than 3.

You can solve an **inequality** the same way you solve an equation. The inequality symbols $<$, $>$, $\ge$, and $\le$ are used to compare expressions.

Solving an Inequality Using Subtraction

Solve and graph the inequality $x + 10 \geq 8$

Step 1: Write the inequality.

$$x + 10 \geq 8$$

Step 2: Subtract 10 from both sides of the inequality.

$$x + \cancel{10} - \cancel{10} \geq 8 - 10$$

Step 3: Write the solution.

$$x \geq {}^-2$$

Step 4: Graph the solution.

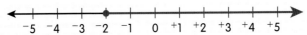

Use a solid circle to graph an inequality that shows less than or equal to ($\leq$) and greater than or equal to ($\geq$). (This solution set does include $^-2$, so the solid circle is used.)

Solve and graph the inequality $x + 15 \leq 20$

Step 1: Write the inequality.

$$x + 15 \leq 20$$

Step 2: Subtract 15 from both sides of the inequality.

$$x + \cancel{15} - \cancel{15} \leq 20 - 15$$

Step 3: Write the solution.

$$x \leq 5$$

Step 4: Graph the solution.

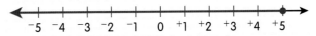

To review the meanings of **inequality symbols**, see page 40.

Solving inequalities using multiplication or division is similar to solving algebraic equations. There is only one exception.

If you multiply or divide both sides of an inequality by a negative number, you have to reverse the direction of the inequality symbol.

If the original inequality is $<$, change the direction to $>$. If the original inequality is $>$, change the direction to $<$.

Solve $\dfrac{n}{-6} > 3$

Step 1: Write the inequality. $\qquad \dfrac{n}{-6} > 3$

Step 2: Multiply both sides of the inequality by $^-6$. $\qquad ^-6 \times \dfrac{n}{-6} > 3 \times {}^-6$

Step 3: Change the direction of the inequality sign. $\qquad \dfrac{^-6}{1} \times \dfrac{n}{^-6} < 3 \times {}^-6$

Step 4: Write the solution. $\qquad n < {}^-18$

Solve $\dfrac{n}{6} > 3$

Step 1: Write the inequality. $\qquad \dfrac{n}{6} > 3$

Step 2: Multiply both sides of the inequality by 6. $\qquad 6 \times \dfrac{n}{6} > 3 \times 6$

Step 3: Write the solution. $\qquad n > 18$

When you multiply or divide both sides of an inequality by a negative number, switch the direction of the inequality symbol.

Solving Inequalities Using Division

To solve an inequality using division:

1. Divide both sides of the inequality by the number that the variable is being multiplied by.
2. If you divide both sides of the inequality by a negative number, reverse the direction of the inequality sign.

Solve $-5n < -20$

Step 1: Write the inequality.

$$-5n < -20$$

Step 2: Divide both sides of the inequality by -5.

$$\frac{-5n}{-5} < \frac{-20}{-5}$$

Step 3: Change the direction of the inequality sign.

$$\frac{-\cancel{5}n}{-\cancel{5}} > \frac{-20}{-5}$$

Step 4: Write the solution.

$$n > 4$$

Solve $5n < -20$

Step 1: Write the inequality.

$$5n < -20$$

Step 2: Divide both sides of the inequality by 5.

$$\frac{\cancel{5}n}{\cancel{5}} < \frac{-20}{5}$$

Step 3: Write the solution.

$$n < -4$$

When you multiply or divide both sides of an inequality by a positive number, the direction of the inequality remains the same.

Further Reading

Books

Downing, Douglas A. *Algebra, The Easy Way.* Hauppauge, New York: Barron Educational Series, Inc., 2003.

Zegarelli, Mark. *Basic Math and Pre Algebra Workbook for Dummies.* New Jersey: Wiley Publishing Inc., 2008.

Internet Addresses

Education 4 Kids. *Math Flashcards to Kids.* ©1995–2005. <http://www.edu4kids.com/index.php?TB=2&page=12>.

Manura, David. *Math2.org.* ©1995–2005. <http://www.math2.org/>.

The Math Forum. *Ask Dr. Math.* © 1994–2004. <http://mathforum.org/dr.math/>.

National Council of Teachers of Mathematics. *Figure This! Math Challenges for Families.* ©1999. <http://www.figurethis.org/index.html>.

Index